Network Ma
For Introverts

Guide To Success For The Shy Network Marketer

www.NetworkMarketingKingdom.com

© Copyright 2015 by NetworkMarketingKingdom.com- All rights reserved.

Bonus Video: How To Get Leads and Customers Online

Subscribe To Get Free Tips On How To Generate Leads and Get Customers

When you subscribe to get network marketing tips via email, you will get free access to exclusive subscriber-only resources. All you have to do is enter your email address to get instant access.

These resources will help you get more out of your business – to be able to reach your goals, have more motivation, be at your best, and live the life you've always dreamed of. I'm always adding new resources, which you will be notified of as a subscriber. These will help you get an endless amount of leads and customers.

Visit http://www.networkmarketingkingdom.com/video to Acces The Bonus Video

Table Of Contents

Introduction

Chapter 1: How Introversion Impacts Your Business

Chapter 2: Alternative Strategies to Get Results

Chapter 3: Stepping Out Of Your Comfort Zone

Chapter 4: Build Your Team and Being a Leader

Chapter 5: Confidence Building

Chapter 6: Creating Goals and a Plan for Success

Conclusion

Introduction

First off, thank you for reading this book. I see that you're a person that likes to take action. As we know, investing in ourselves pays off ten fold in the future, if the information you read is implemented.

Not just financially, but invest in your education so you can <u>learn more and earn more</u>. In turn, you can inspire others to do the same by becoming a great leader. People look up to those who are courageous, inspiring, and adds value to their lives. When I think back, most of the people I looked up to were those getting results and sharing what they did to get those results.

In network marketing, we have to work on our self-growth, invest in ourselves, and create connections with others in order to be successful.

Most of the top leaders are looked up to because they were courageous, they put themselves out there and got out of their comfort zone. This is what this book is about. It's about shifting your mindset and realizing why you tend to sabotage your success by not going after what you want.

Let's get this straight: I'm not trying to change you. I'm simply giving you resources to make you a better you. My goal is to inspire you to become more of who you truly want to be.

Anyone can be successful at network marketing who is willing to put in the work and follow the system. No matter if they're shy, or if they're outgoing. The great thing about this industry is how much self-growth that comes along with it. It's the one business that will help you become more disciplined, social, business minded, and motivated.

I also want to say, be who you are. Although you may be an introvert, I'm sure there's more to your personality. Always be yourself. As introverts, we tend to loosen up once we get to know people better-- but in this business when you're talking to strangers it can be hard to express who we truly are and our personality upon meeting someone.

Getting out there and meeting new people is how we grow. All we need is the courage to take the first step. The first step by pressing publish on that YouTube video, or approaching that person at a networking event. Once get the courage to take action in spite of our fears, we become better network marketers, better team leaders, and better people.

The truth is, you don't have to be an outgoing socialite to make money with network marketing. People will buy from you and join your team once they trust you. But the only way to build trust is to start building networks. Build trust by being consistent, taking action, and having outstanding customer service. Go above and beyond for your team and customers, and you'll find yourself developing confidence and freedom.

About Me

— google / facebook

My name is Argena Olivis and I was in network marketing for a while and had success despite my introversion. Although I am shy, I'm always working on my mindset and getting out of my comfort zone.

I am an avid learner, I've taken many courses and read many books on network marketing. There was no secret to my success, I just worked hard, kept learning, and took action.

It was also fun to take people that were in the same company as me on my journey to success in that company. I started off in internet marketing, but came across the opportunity and gave it a shot.

I have never been outgoing, but I made it a mission to become successful regardless. On my journey, by putting myself out there, going to meetings, events, etc. I was able to meet great mentors, make friends, and develop an online presence.

You can do the same, you can be an <u>introvert and still</u> make money in your network marketing company. You can still have lots of customers and team members, even though you don't really like to be the center of attention. And I'm going to show you exactly how to do so.

Chapter 1: How Introversion Impacts Your Business

You may have never thought about it, but your personality does have a big impact on your business. It has an impact on the amount of success you have or don't have.

The way you are, the way you see things, the way you talk to people, and what you're willing to do versus the next network marketer can create a big divide in your success versus theirs.

You may be working twice as hard for fewer results. But did you ever think to yourself: "If I was more outgoing and wasn't afraid to reach out to more people than I would have a bigger team or bigger customer base." I know I've had these feelings.

Those moments where you think about sharing your business opportunity, but never speak up. Or those moments where you're too afraid to make calls and follow up with others. As introverts, some things just scare the hell out of us and we just don't want to do them.

But as we push through and try to change ourselves, it only creates more stress on us and our business. While you should do something every day that scares you, sometimes these big steps can come off as desperate and in the end, we can lose respect and trust with friends and family who just weren't open, and now look at us in a different way—all because we tried to "get out there and be bold".

Some things are just not for us, some things are not in our personality. That's why I wrote this book because the fact is, you can have success with network marketing. It may take a little more work, but it's absolutely worth it.

In this book, I will not try to change you. You are who you are. My goal here is to get you to look at this business a little differently. I want you to see what options you have. I want you to find ways where you can recruit reps and get customers without being out of character.

About Introverts

In order to be a better network marketer, you need to learn more about yourself. The more you know about yourself, the better you can serve others. As we already know, you're an introvert. But you need to know exactly what an introvert is so you can maximize your strengths.

Studies show that everyone has a little of both introversion and extraversion in them. But we tend to lean more towards one or the other.

Quiet

Introverts are quiet. I know I'm quiet. Growing up I was never the one to participate in group discussions, I liked to take it all in. This didn't mean I wasn't learning or that I wasn't interested in the subject; It just meant I either didn't have an opinion at the time, or there are too many people talking loudly for me to feel comfortable enough to express how I was feeling.

I was so shy in these discussions that I always over-thought. I was thinking about what I could say to add to the discussion, what people would think about me, if I would sound stupid if I said something. Also, it seems like the extroverts always took my answers first, and I never got a chance to speak up.

Then a group leader or teacher would ask me if I had something to add, I could've regurgitated what everyone else had said, but I felt I would sound stupid because it wouldn't be original.

Maybe some of these traits go along with being confident too. Sometimes if you're not confident, you'll always be too afraid to share how you really feel or add to a discussion.

But the thing is...I'm not quiet, and I was never quiet. I was just quiet in groups and discussions. If I get to know and trust that I could be myself around someone; you can't get me to shut up. It just takes me longer to warm up to new people. So in turn they think I'm quiet, but really I just don't have anything to say until I can get to know you and trust you a little more.

Being quiet can definitely impact your business. If you need time to gain trust and get to know someone before approaching them, did you ever think maybe they're the same way?

Sometimes you have to not think about business, but think about how you can build relationships first. Before approaching someone, think about how you can add value to them first. This will put your mind at ease, and also make it easier for you to approach others. Come from a mindset of a giver, and you have no reason to be shy.

When you approach someone, the other person expects you to do all the talking. This can make things awkward really fast if you're a quiet person who doesn't have a lot to say. You know what gets rid of shyness? Practice.

Practice what you're going to say to a person. You can do it with a trusted spouse or friend.

So here's the solution: Practice what you're going to say, but don't get too caught up on the word for word, and come from a place where you'll be adding value to them and giving them something. Think about building a relationship, not about growing your team.

Before you know it, you'll have lots of new associates and possible business partners or customers in the future. Even if they're not interested, the great thing about networking is they may know someone who is.

You can't really get over being quiet. It's you, it's who you are. But you can practice adding to discussions and focus more on how you can add to the group. And there will come times when you literally don't have anything to possibly add or say. Don't stress about this, just do what you can and say what you can at the time. Don't worry about what others will think or you'll drive yourself crazy.

Put your focus on warming up to the group, in time speaking up will come more naturally. Once you get to know a few more people, you'll be more comfortable sharing.

Know that you're quiet and own it. Know that you're not quiet around those you know well, and that you're working on getting to know others better before putting your whole self out there.

Being Alone

If you like to be alone, this can impact your business; but of course, there're ways to work around it.

Having time to yourself can be a good thing in network

Advantages/strengths of being introvert have a look at my posts - MBTI.

marketing. This time alone gives you time to brainstorm business ideas, set goals, work on your mindset, study the business, and market your business both online and offline.

Sometimes we just don't feel like being around others; it can truly drain our energy. But we can use this time to be productive instead of feeling bad about it. We can practice for an upcoming webinar or conference call we're hosting, we can send out thank you cards to our team and our customers. The possibilities are endless.

Do not feel bad when you want to be alone. Everyone needs a break. We just need more breaks than others to really be in peace with ourselves and think about what's going on. Embrace who you are and how you're feeling at the moment.

But when you start longing for a connection, make sure to call a friend or family remember to spend time with. Being alone for too long can often result in depression, we do need that human interaction to pump us up and make us feel good sometimes.

Sometimes you don't have to be physically alone, sometimes you feel alone in a crowd or a group. This means you haven't connected with anyone on a deep level the way we like to do. When this happens—simply go with the flow. Don't try to force anything because you may regret it later.

It may be harder for you to make friends and make connections, but once you do, you won't feel alone; you'll feel like you've met someone who you can trust and stick with for as long as possible.

Feeling like you're alone in a crowd can impact your business. You may get depressive thoughts or feel like you're left out. But once you realize that you're just being yourself and you can't force anything then you'll be okay.

If you truly hate this feeling, or if you hate being alone; avoid the stress of it. This means bringing someone along with you that you know or working on your communication skills so you can make new connections quickly.

Everything takes time. Once you know what you need to work on you'll feel more comfortable and confident being alone or learn how to avoid being alone. The choice is yours, don't let anyone else make it for you.

Small Talk *FORM - possibly*

<u>Introverts do not like small talk</u>. They like deeper connections and talking about things meaningful to them.

Not enjoying small talk can definitely impact your business; network marketing is a people business. This means it's based on making connections, meeting a lot of new people, and being able to start conversations with strangers.

The answer to this is simple. Learn how you can make small talk more enjoyable. One way to make it more enjoyable is to lead the small talk in the direction you want it to go. This requires skills; <u>leadership and communication skills</u>.

There is a strategy out there for anything you want to accomplish, you just have to believe it works and put what you learn into action. So if you don't enjoy small talk, it's not the end of the world. All you have to do is make it a better situation for yourself, and then it becomes a win-win situation.

Balance of Business, Social, and Solitude

As introverts, we need our solitude. We need time to recharge from a lot of excitement and from the energy that others may take from us. Your business may try to interfere with your need for solitude, but don't let it.

This time is very important for you and it will keep you balanced and in the game longer. So make sure that you always have some time to reflect and be alone throughout the day.

Although it may be tempting, you don't want to be alone all the time. Plan for some social events, either in business or with family and friends. It's always refreshing to have something to look forward to throughout the week.

Set your schedule up so you can have a nice balance of being in solitude, network and socializing, and working on your business. This will keep things more exciting for you; which in turn will help your business and personal life.

When Prospects Reach Out

A lot of times, introverts don't have the energy to take surprise calls. Sometimes, though, we can get in the mood to be social. Most likely you'll be getting calls about your business opportunity throughout the day.

Sometimes you just won't be in the mood to take the call. And it may be a hot lead on the other line, as you already know, prospects tend to lose enthusiasm about the business after a certain period of time, so answering your phone is extremely important.

You need to answer the phone, but make sure to have a system for it. Make sure you set something up where you

[handwritten: need to think about phone leave message]

get in a certain state and mindset while talking to potential recruits and customers.

When you don't feel like answering the phone, here are some ideas:

- Visualize the reason you want to be successful (new house, new car, your kids, etc.)
- Smile (really big)
- Think of it as a close friend calling that's in an emergency
- Make it a fun experience by being yourself, don't feel like you have to say fancy words or sell anyone

Using these physical triggers will make answering the phone more enjoyable, and you'll be able to be more successful in the long run.

Don't Like People

Since introverts are not outgoing, people tend to get the idea that they don't like people. But this is far from the truth. The truth is you do like people, you just don't like to be around them for long periods of time because it drains your energy.

Don't feel bad if you need time alone, in your heart you know that it's not true that you "don't like people", you're just different, and there's nothing wrong with that. If everyone were the same, this would be one boring world.

If people are trying to communicate with you and you find it awkward, of course, this can impact your business. But being too perfect and polished is not a good thing either because people won't trust you as much.

People do want to see confidence in you so that they know you believe in what you're selling; so the best thing to do is practice and rehearse what you will say to people before approaching them.

The most successful marketers are always being themselves, they are comfortable in their own bodies, and they don't need to please anyone. Just think about how you can help others, come from a place of servitude. If you do that, you won't have to worry about people thinking you don't like them.

Comfort Zone

Most introverts are people of habit and routine and they really don't enjoy trying new things. At times, they can be adventurous, but most of the time, we know what we like and we keep doing what keeps us comfortable and feeling safe.

Everyone gets shy, everyone has a mind that holds them back from being successful, so introverts are not alone. What happens is when we try to do new things, our mind stops us. It's a defense mechanism we have, our minds are simply trying to keep us safe.

But the ones who can go beyond their minds, and condition their minds for greater things are the ones who are growing. Your goal should always be to grow as a person.

Growing comes with overcoming fears, getting out of your comfort zone, and simply doing things you're afraid to do. Without growth within yourself, there is not growth for your business.

Small Network

As an introvert, you probably have come across a lot of people who you would not consider a friend but an associate. Introverts typically have small networks of friends and family that can be trusted.

With a small network, this impacts your business negatively. In the next chapter, we'll be discussing how you can connect with more people and grow your network without necessarily having to be someone you're not.

Outgoing

No, you're most likely not outgoing if you're reading this book. But you don't have to be outgoing to be successful. There are other strategies you can use to grow your business without always taking the microphone, having something to say, giving public speeches, or being the first one to volunteer for something.

Believe it or not, some people find more comfort and trust in someone who is a great listener rather than a big talker. Although it is necessary to grow, you don't have to do things you don't enjoy just to find acceptance.

Many people will appreciate you for sticking to your guns, for not always being on level ten, and for not always trying to slick talk someone into something.

Just as long as you're outgoing in the aspect of customer service and helping your team, that's all you'll need to be a great network marketer.

Groups

I've personally been put into a lot of situations where I'm in a group and I literally can't think of anything to add to the conversation. So people automatically will think you're quiet or that you don't want to participate.

The best way to handle this is just speaking when spoken to, if they ask if you have anything to add simply tell the truth. It's okay, it's not the end of the world.

If you do have something to add to the group but you're too shy; then speak up. I know it will take stepping out to your comfort zone, but it's worth it. Make it a habit to start speaking up for yourself. This can be critical to your success; not only in business, but in general. Try to keep your emotions out of it.

I only like to talk if I have something to say. I don't like small talk, and I don't want to say just anything in order to please others. Stick to what you believe in, if you don't have anything to add then that's just fine.

It's known that introverts like to have deeper conversations and connections. These connections don't typically happen in groups, and if you're in a group you're probably being exposed to small talk. So make the best of it, share what you have and keep it moving.

Confrontation

Confrontation is something that introverts hate. This can also impact your business. Sometimes our emotions get involved and we feel like we're being attacked.

Keep in mind that we have picked a business that deals a lot with confrontation and rejection. Things will get uncomfortable very quickly.

The best way to handle confrontation; rather it's a troll that talks down on your company or the industry, a person who dislikes your YouTube video, or someone who puts you down on social media—is to simply take that person out of your world.

This means deleting or blocking a person right away, not responding to negative reviews, and not tolerating disrespect. Get these people out of your life and fast.

If you're feeling down or overwhelmed by a situation, the best thing to do is to remember the great things. Keep your great customers and team members in mind. Don't allow someone to come in and change your feelings about yourself or what you're doing.

Seek support from others and confide in a trusted friend. Don't let these small things keep you down, you have too much work to do.

You can't avoid confrontation. You have to stand up for what you believe; that's what people will respect about you and follow you for. So it's best to deal with it in a classy way that doesn't get you out of character, which isn't good for business.

Let people have their opinions, people get upset when they feel they can't voice how they feel. Just let it go, and let it be.

Benefits of Being an Introvert

Although a lot of negativity can be associated with introversion; people need introverts. We are not the majority, but we are here making a difference. Introverts are great listeners, great at building trust, easy to approach, and they choose their words carefully.

Great Listeners

Some love to talk, others are great listeners. Great listeners, like us introverts, can come in handy. When you listen to others, it makes them feel good and it also builds trust.

This is definitely a beneficial trait that can impact your business in a positive way. Just keep in mind to remember what people have said to you; if you not only listen, but you remember, you will easily win people over.

When listening to prospects, make sure to take note of their concerns, goals, and other important information. It really feels good when someone actually remembers you and what you want on a deep level. This is also great for accountability for team members.

When listening to a mentor, actually take their advice and give them credit for any results you've gotten.

Listening can be a powerful tool that you have the benefit of doing very well naturally. Embrace your listening skills and make it something great.

Building Trust

Because introverts don't easily let people in, they tend to be more trustworthy since they're not so open with everyone.

People tend to avoid people that are super outgoing when it comes to their secrets. I know I don't want to tell my business to someone who is always running their mouth.

So when you look at it, people are more likely to put their trust in introverts because of their great listening skills and their "quiet" ways.

So use this to your advantage. Let people know they can trust you by keeping their secrets, and listening to them.

Easy To Approach

I don't know about you, but if someone is really wild by nature and over confident, I tend to avoid approaching them because of their super high energy doesn't match mines.

People are more likely to approach people that are alone, and that seem to be good listeners. People seek quiet and shy people to connect with, especially if they have some of the same characteristics.

But at the end of the day, opposites attract; so you may find yourself in a relationship or in a friendship with an extrovert. Either way, you seem low key and easily approachable, so use this to your advantage.

Be helpful. Helpful people seem to be approached the most. Be transparent when adding value and teaching; this will automatically draw people to you.

Choose Words Carefully

Introverts don't typically just say what comes to their minds. They usually think it over before speaking. They usually prepare what they will say to avoid any confrontation or bad feedback.

This is a good trait. Sometimes there are some things you just can't take back. Being a person who thinks things through can save you a lot of stress and trouble in the future.

It also helps your confidence to prepare what you're going to say so you can be less stressed and share how you feel in a way that you see fit.

Because you think before you speak; you most likely have less enemies and more relationships that can be built.

Usually introverts choose their words carefully around strangers. When you get around your family or friends, it may be a whole different story depending on your personality. When introverts develop a comfort around someone, they're more likely to share how the feel more openly without much thought.

The Take Away

We've gone over some great things in this chapter. This chapter was designed to help you learn more about yourself and introversion and give you a few pointers on how it can impact your business in both a negative and positive way.

You should never try to change you who you are, but you should be willing to grow. Become more aware of who you are and look toward who you're working to become.

Embrace your flaws and your talents, they are what make you unique. You can be successful at network marketing even if you're not outgoing.

Chapter 2: Alternative Strategies to Get Results

Yes, the old network marketing strategies still work; which include things that require you to get outside your comfort zone such as: going door to door, approaching anyone within ten feet of you, recruiting family and friends, and running hotel meetings about your opportunity.

But it's a new day, now other things work just as well, if not better, with the power of the internet. The internet works so well that some network marketing companies are completely internet based.

So don't get stuck in the mindset that you'll have to talk to complete strangers one on one. You don't have to do any of that and you can still be successful if you have the right systems set up. That's what we're going to be talking about in the coming chapters.

Internet Marketing

Internet marketing is just in its beginning stages. More and more people are shopping online, getting recruits online, and building their empire online. You can do it too, but it takes hard work, consistency, patience, and commitment.

The great thing about using the internet is you can get prospects, customers, or new business partners 24/7. As you already know, network marketing is based on getting new leads. The best ways to do this is through: writing books, blog posts, videos, social media, podcasts, conference calls, and email marketing.

First you have to decide which strategy you want to start working on. Choose one or two things that you will do online to bring in new leads on a consistent basis. Notice how I said: bring in. This means most of the times the leads will come to you after you've added value to their lives and inspired them.

Writing Books

My guess is, you've been reading a lot about network marketing. Since you're reading this book; you most likely are one of the people who invest in themselves and their business regularly. This means you've been taking in a lot of information.

You don't have to be an expert to write a book; you just have to know more than the next person. The reasons I'm suggesting you write a book is:
- Creditability
- New Passive Income Stream
- Exposure
- Lead Generation
- Etc.

You may be thinking that you don't even know what you'd write a book about. Well, what products is you company based around? Makeup? Weight Loss? Travel? Whatever your company's product is; you can write a book about that topic. I'm assuming since you're in the company you know a thing or two about it.

Right now, the Kindle eBook publishing space is blowing up. But you're not writing to be in competition with anyone; you're writing a book in order to be able to stand out from all the other network marketers out there.

Think about it, most people won't take action on this advice. It may sound good to them, but they'll self-sabotage themselves and not do anything. Don't be the majority; stick out and do what no one else is willing to do.

I go through a step by step process on how to create your first kindle book here:
http://www.argenaolivis.com/freekindlecourse

and the great thing about it is you can easily make your kindle book a paperback book, here're the instructions on creating a paperback book:
http://www.argenaolivis.com/createsapcecourse

Once you complete your first book, you'll feel very accomplished and it's something that you can mention you've done. This will give you more creditability, and people will see you as an executor. They'll look up to you and inspire to do great things, just like you.

Another great thing about this is the leads it will bring in. You'll be utilizing Amazon's traffic to get new leads daily. Believe it or not, you can actually have your book so it's permanently free. This will help you to generate leads on a consistent basis.

Use the book writing strategy as a way to tell the world that you can add value and that you know your stuff. Go out there and get some results so you can teach your methods with other people. The more people you help, the more your team and customer base will grow.

You want to focus on activities that generate the greatest return on your investment, the ones that help you reach the most people that you don't have to keep doing over and over again. A book will help you to accomplish this.

Your book can also help you to get exposure on podcasts, shows, etc. People will see you as an expert and may want to interview you; which in turn will allow you to get in front of more audiences and grow your own audience simultaneously.

Blogging

Although blogging may be a little saturated from the make money standpoint; it's still necessary for a business owner such as yourself. People need a hub where they can get in contact with you and check out more of what you have to offer.

Your company most likely has provided you with a cookie-cutter blog that they give to all their distributors; do not put your time into that site. The only time you want to recommend this site is when you're sending someone to shop or sign up.

You want to brand yourself. You have a few options. You can create a website about your company, a team website, or a website about the product that your company sells. You want to invest money in building your own website because it looks more professional.

Here is step by step instructions on how to create a website:
http://www.networkmarketingkingdom.com/website/

You don't have to blog at all. Your website should be there to capture leads. You want to funnel traffic to your blog and in turn, capture leads. You do this through email marketing. We will talk about email marketing a little later.

The pages you must have on your site: contact, links to your company website (for new customers or sign ups), about me, products you offer, any upcoming events you may be hosting, links to connect on social media, etc.

You can also offer different training on your website that will add value to potential leads. The possibilities are endless; don't get too overwhelmed, simply create the basic pages and you can go from there. But this is something you need to build an online presence.

Make sure you tell others about your website on social media and put it on your business cards. Not having only the cookie-cutter website will help you to stand out from the crowd.

*** Expert Tip: Buy an easy to remember domain name and have it forwarded to the website your company provides you with. This will help you to stand out as well.

If you really want to make blogging a lead generator for you; it won't be easy, but it'll be worth it. You will spend a lot of time writing and providing value and you may not get many readers, at first, depending on how you market your blog.

Just remember to brush up on your search engine optimization (SEO) skills. Blogging can also create other income streams for you. Keep that in mind.

Video Marketing

I know that most introverts do not like doing videos because of the exposure you can get and really putting yourself out there may be super uncomfortable. Although I didn't like the feeling when I started doing videos, I managed to make them anyway.

The best thing you can do is practice. Most people are more worried about the value you will be adding to their lives; they're not worried about you pronouncing words correctly or what you look like in your videos. You don't even have to show your face in videos, you can record your screen by using tools such as Screen-Cast-O-Matic.com or Jing.

But it's nice to have at least one video that shows your face, so your audience can know what you look like, and trust you more by being able to look you in the eyes. Another great thing about video creation is you're able to practice and prepare before releasing it out into the world.

I think video should be on the top of your list for alternative strategies to get leads online. This is because it's so many people aren't doing videos and it's an amazing way to connect with new people and network online. Creating a YouTube channel is a way to stand out from the crowd.

Just get started. Start creating videos around topics that you know well and are relevant to your target market in order to generate leads. In your video description, make sure to link by to your blog or company website. Also, make sure to send people to your squeeze page in order to get leads on your email list.

Here are some ideas on the types of videos to create for your channel:
- product reviews
- motivational videos and breakthroughs
- case studies
- help with network marketing
- help with whatever product your company sells

This will be a step out of your comfort zone; but if you're constantly providing value and are consistent with posting and marketing your videos by using the right keywords, then you're bound to get results. These results will consist of new team members and or customers.

The goal of your videos should be to be helpful and solve the problems that your customer and potential team members may have.

Get started with video as soon as possible, even if it's just recording your screen.

I repeat, this is the way to get ahead of your competition. By doing video, people will get a better gist of your personality, which would otherwise be more difficult in a group setting.

Social Media

Social media does include sites like YouTube, but also other sites that may be great for your business are: Facebook, Pinterest, Twitter, Instagram, and Linked In. These are sites that already have a lot of traffic, and if you can get in there and leverage that traffic it can do wonders for your business. But to be successful on social media takes a lot of patience, commitment, and time.

***Expert Tip: Consider using the ads feature on these social media platforms. Learn how to get paid traffic from social media to your blog and other products. This skill will help you to become an expert on how much it costs to get a lead. Don't just throw money away. Invest in courses that teach you how to get paid traffic from these sites. Most people are looking to get free traffic, but paid social media traffic gives you more control.

Facebook

Facebook is an obvious platform you should be on. You most likely already have a fan page already. The biggest key to Facebook success is building relationships and, in turn, generating leads.

You can do this by sharing valuable tips that are relevant to your business opportunity. It's also a great place for announcements.

A part of Facebook that is underutilized and can make a big difference in your business is Facebook groups. You can create a group around whatever topic you want. The great thing about this is you can filter who you let into the group.

Having a private Facebook group for your <u>team, prospects,</u> <u>clients</u> and people interested in the industry is a way for introverts to create leverage and make connections without having to get too out of their comfort zone.

Pinterest

Pinterest is another alternative way to market your business and generate new leads. Keep in mind that Pinterest is mainly used by women. So if you have a product or service that is geared toward women, Pinterest is the perfect place to start.

Pinterest is an image-based social media website that you're able to create different boards on different topics. You're also able to "repin" others pins. You can create some images using programs like www.pickmonkey.com or www.canva.com.

You can also make a business account on Pinterest. Make sure to do this and verify your website. Also, make sure to use hashtags in your description to get your pins more exposure. In the description of your pins, add a link by to your website or your distributor website.

You're able to post YouTube videos on Pinterest as well. All in all, Pinterest is a highly trafficked social media platform that you can utilize to build leads while still building trust with prospects.

Twitter

Twitter is right behind Facebook as far as the amount of users and traffic. So it's definitely a social media platform where you can market to your audience.

Twitter is a place where you can find out real-time information. You can see what people are talking about now and what's trending by simply typing in search terms. This is great news for you, because you can use this to do research and connect with prospects.

Just like any other platform, you want to make sure you're adding value through tips; the only difference is your tips have to be 140 characters or less. Similar to Pinterest, you want to use hashtags in order to get more exposure to your tweets.

You can find prospects by using Twitter search to look up different keywords. Say for instance your company sells weight loss products: You can do a search in twitter for the keyword "weight" and see what people are saying. You may just come across someone that is talking about how they need to lose weight. In this situation, you could either mention that person on Twitter by using their Twitter name and ask them if they'd like a free sample of your product, or you can private message them, and ask if it's okay to send them a free sample. This is one way to connect with prospects.

And if they happen to check out your Twitter page to find out more information about you and your product, make sure you're ready. These means have the blog set up professionally. Show that you have helpful tweets going out consistently and that you can be trusted.

Your social media will be the first impression they have of you, so make it worth their while. When reaching out to others, make sure to come from a place of trying to add value and give, have a servant heart; and never worry about what's in it for you. If you have this mindset, you will be much more successful.

Instagram

Instagram is owned by Facebook and is the fastest growing new social media platform. A lot of people are on it, and there's a lot of exposure your business can get there.

Instagram is similar to Pinterest. It's an image based site, but both men and women use it equally. In your Instagram bio, you're able to add one clickable link, make this count. I usually use this to link back to my squeeze page to generate leads.

Use hashtags to get exposure for your pictures. Use the description to explain your image. Creating a description for your images on Instagram can be annoying because you have to type it all out on your phone. That's why I usually create a description and then copy and paste it into Instagram to save time.

Do not put hashtags in your photo's description. Put hashtags in a comment right underneath the photo. It will have the same effect as putting them in the description. The reason you don't want to put them in the description is because once you put those hashtags there, you can't go back and edit them.

When posting, use the location banner to post a call to action. This can be things like "click the link in bio" or "free webinar 8 pm link in bio".

Linked In

Last but not least, we have Linked In. Linked In is a more professional site that you can find a lot of business people. You can use it to make business connections.

You can find people with similar interest and connect with them. You're also able to create groups, so make sure to take advantage of that.

The Takeaway on Social Media

Keep in mind that you only want to master one platform at a time. Consider learning how to get paid traffic from these sites and use them as an alternative strategy to generate leads.

Many introverts can benefit from building their business online. Not only can you make a larger impact but it'll most likely be an experience that makes you happier and that you'll stick with for a longer period of time, opposed to doing traditional marketing which can drain a lot of your energy.

Regardless of what platform you decide to focus on. Make sure to be consistent and post things like:
- upcoming events
- lifestyle pictures
- giveaways
- helpful and valuable tips
- videos
- free gifts
- links to your squeeze page
- etc.

Think of yourself as if you were in your customers shoes, before posting anything think if it's something that that you would want to see on social media.

To learn more about internet marketing for network marketers, check out my book <u>Internet Marketing For Network Marketers: How To Create Automated Systems To Get Recruits and Customers Online</u>

Podcasts

Podcasting today is now very popular. People listen to podcasts on the go while working out, one their way to work, while doing chores, etc. Just think, listening to hours of someone consistently adding value will help you to build trust and, in turn, become more successful in your company.

Create a podcast around what you sell or <u>network marketing in general</u>. Either one of these will help you reach a larger audience without having to get overwhelmed.

You can have the podcast be just you sharing content, or you can bring on guest and interview them. You don't even have to start from scratch if you have YouTube videos; <u>you can simply use the audio from your YouTube videos and make it a podcast.</u>

Podcasting can also bring in a new income stream for you depending on how many downloads you get per episode. You can bring on sponsors. The possibilities and opportunities are endless.

Conference Calls

As you most likely already know, conference calls are extremely popular in the <u>network marketing industry</u>. This may be a step out of your comfort zone, but the great thing is it's something you can practice with just a small amount of listeners at first in order to get the hang out it.

You can use conference calls to inform and train your team, or to have prospects listen in. Many networkers use tools like conference calls and Google Hangouts as a live way to tell people about their company and in turn, generate leads who may be interested in joining your team.

There are free services you can use such as freeconferencecall.com to set up your meeting. All you have to do is be prepared, know what you want to talk about, and give people a call to action at the end.

Email Marketing
This is a big one, and this is the main alternative strategy that you can use to connect with prospects and team members. If you haven't set up your email list yet visit http://www.argenaolivis.com/email-marketing-101/ for a step by step tutorial on how to get started.

Email is the most secure and profitable way to collect leads online. Your goal should be to funnel all your traffic to your squeeze page. A squeeze page is a simple landing page where the only goal is to get the email address of the prospect.

To get the email address, you want to give something away for free. This is called an opt-in offer. Your free gift's intention is to provide something of value upfront in exchange for an email address. It should be something people are willing to pay for.

You can create a book, video, mini course, printables, checklist, etc. Just make sure whatever you're giving away is relevant to your audience and it's something that they'll want and will be willing to opt in for.

The squeeze page is the main page that you want to send people to. Generating emails will allow you to connect with prospects on another level. You can send them emails that will help them, and in turn, some will help you by joining your team or becoming a customer.

The link to your landing page should be the main link you promote. Email is also a secure method. You can always back up your list, and you are able to email your list just in case something happens or you make any major changes. It's the go-to place for you to contact everyone. It's the one thing you'll own and won't have to worry about it being taken away.

Email is special to people. Once you get someone's email you get closer to them. This means you're able to contact them for almost any reason: new content, conference call times, company updates and changes, etc.

Internet Marketing

If you want to learn more of these strategies on how to build your business online; make sure to start investing in yourself, doing the proper research, and taking action. But remember not to get shiny object syndrome. Focus on one method until you master it, then move to the next.

There are tons of ways to build your business online. This is great for introverts and is something you really want to get into.

Text Messaging and Email

You may not be ready to talk to people over the phone just yet, and that's okay. Take baby steps. The great thing is you decided you want to start a business, and you will grow and get out of your comfort zone as your desire to be successful grows.

If all else fails, and you truly want to connect with others, use text messaging and emails. Although these methods can be less personal, it's better than nothing.

Make sure to craft your emails and texts in a way where you come off as welcoming and eager to help. You'll get better at text and email once you start using them consistently. Create scripts that you use that work best for you, this may take some trial and error before you get the words that work best for you.

How Bad Do You Want Success

Introvert or not, if you don't truly want success badly, then you're not going to be committed and do what it takes to achieve your goals.

It's time to recognize why you joined network marketing in the first place. That reason alone should motivate you to achieve more, but you still need daily inspiration and motivation.

Work on yourself and your personal development. Be the upline you wish you had. This is going to be hard work; you're at a disadvantage if you're not educated about the industry. And you're taking the right steps by reading this book.

Visualize what you want, set goals that will get you there. If you want to be successful you'll do whatever it takes, introvert or not.

Chapter 3: Stepping Out Of Your Comfort Zone

I let you know earlier in the book that I will not try to change you. But I wouldn't be a good friend if I didn't recommend self-growth, and self-growth includes doing things that you're not comfortable with and having different experiences. While you should accept and have confidence in who you are, you should always be striving to become a better person.

Don't Feel Obligated

If you're at an event or doing something out of your comfort zone, don't feel obligated to stay. Leave when you want, you create your life and you always have a choice.

Try Something New Every Day

When we fear something; it's because we fear the unknown. But instead of having anxiety about things, look at them as a fun adventure. Try new things every day, and tell your mind that you're only going to test it out to see how you like it.

This is great for business; it will allow you to see if where you're putting your efforts and the results you'll get from those efforts.

For example: I was super afraid to do YouTube videos, but I still started making YouTube videos that solved problems for people in my particular company. In time, I saw results, so I kept going.

Despite my fear, I still took action and now that channel

consistently helps me to connect with people in that company, and it also brings in leads that may be looking to join my team.

Events and Meetings

Although you may not like group settings, I still recommend you go to events and meetings that your company or upline holds. This will show you dedication and will also inspire you and give you new ideas and updates on how to improve your business.

I doubt if anyone will have you speak at an event, the worse that can happen is at a meeting they may ask you to introduce yourself or share something with the group.

Know What to Say

There's a famous quote by Benjamin Franklin that I always loved: "By failing to prepare, you're preparing to fail".

I love this because it pretty much sums up how introverts can be prepared for almost anything by practicing.

This means using and memorizing relevant scripts, knowing what to say or do, knowing all the possible outcomes, accepting that people may say yes or no, and working on your mindset to quickly get over rejection or the fear of rejection.

Having a Business Friend

Make a friend in the business, this can be a downline member or even your upline. This will hold you accountable for going to events, and also make you feel more comfortable talking to others.

Work to develop a deeper friendship with someone in

the business so you can have these benefits.

Using the Phone

If you have a lot of anxiety when it comes to reaching out to people, then it's time to set your business up to where you have people calling you instead. You can do this by using attraction marketing.

Attraction marketing is when people are drawn to you and inspired by your story, and, in turn, they want to become more like you, so they tend to follow you. You can be an attraction marketer by using the internet for leverage and encouraging people to call you. Keep in mind that people are attracted to those that are helpful and are getting the results that they themselves want.

When you do answer the phone, be prepared. Make sure you're in control of the conversation. Keep in mind that preparation increases confidence.

Making Breakthroughs

As you continue to learn and grow you'll find that you'll begin to make breakthroughs in your business. You make breakthroughs when you finally get out there and do something you've never done or that you've been afraid to do.

To set yourself up to have breakthroughs, you have to put yourself out there. You'll be surprised at the results you get when you do something you've never done or that you've been afraid to do.

A fact that I learned over time is that no one is worried about you. That's right, now one really cares that you just walked into the room or that you're posting videos on YouTube. Don't be selfish, everything is not about you. People have lives to live and if you think someone is always worried about you, it's in your head.

People are going to be people. Yes, they may say things about you behind your back, or sometimes even to your face. But it's very rare. Don't let what you think people will think hold you back. If all it takes to get you to give up on what you want to do is a little confrontation, then maybe this business isn't for you.

Sometimes you have to sacrifice for what you want, especially when you're asking for a lot. When it comes down to it, you have to either sink or swim. Don't sink, challenge yourself and work on your confidence.

Chapter 4: Build Your Team and Being a Leader

Introverts make good leaders. This is because they are easy to confide in, great listeners, and think things through thoroughly before making a decision for their team.

How to Motivate Other Introverts on Your Team

You know your team members best, so if you see that someone is a little shy and quiet; they're most likely an introvert like you. Let these people be who they are; if you try to push them too hard, you may never see them again.

Just like you, they need time to get to know you and develop a relationship with you before they can trust you fully and take direction from you. So work on building a relationship with those types of team members. This special attention will keep them loyal to you and as a result, you'll be helping them to grow as a person as you grow yourself.

Don't try to call them out during any meetings or events; they won't like that because they don't like being put on the spot. Introverts like to observe and take in information before doing anything.

If you're going to confront them do it one on one, so you can continue building that relationship and rapport with them. People like to feel important, remember that; it'll make you a better leader.

The best way to motivate and introvert is to show them the results you've gotten, and help them to believe that they too can get these results. Show them exactly how you do things and let them make their own way to becoming successful.

Let Your Team Motivate You

Your team will motivate you to keep going. You have to lead by example. If you want your team to be great, you have to be great. Don't expect or ask them to things that you don't do yourself.

Your team will follow you. If they see that you're becoming successful by hosting conference calls, they're start hosting conference calls. You want them to follow the leader, but first make sure the leader is doing what they need to do to set a good example.

Lead by example. If your team did exactly what you do on a daily basis, how would their results be?

Communication

You want to have great communication with your team. Make sure that everyone is on the same page. Keep in mind that if someone doesn't know what's expected of them, they can't make any changes.

Constantly communicate with your team, let them know any updates or things that are happening. Don't leave anyone in the dark that doesn't want to be there. Be clear and intentional about what you want and what you expect.

Set sales and recruiting goals, so your team knows exactly what to strive for. And have training readily available to them so they always know what to do.

Team Site and Facebook Group

Create a website for your team. This can be a private or a public site that your team can access to get the information and training they need.

If you want to make the site private, you can set up a regular WordPress site and then from there you can add a plugin called s2member. This will give access to only certain people.

Having a private site will give your team members a sense of belonging, consider letting them add their team members and downline to the site too. People love exclusivity and it's something special you can create for your team to give them training and so they can connect with each other.

You can also have the site open to all, or have some content available to all and some only for team members. It's completely up to you. There are also benefits to having it be an open site. The open site will attract more leads who will want to join your team if they see some of your training and they think you can help them get what they want.

Also, create a closed Facebook group where everyone can post updates, questions, etc. This will help to build a community among team members.

Attraction Marketing

You want people to be attracted to you. This will help you to grow and become a better networker. Think about what attracts you to other successful leaders in the industry.

What attracts you to them? It's most likely their confidence, their results, the value they share, their lifestyle, and maybe even the way they look. To truly be successful, you have to find out how you can start to have and portray the things that the top leaders have.

So start developing your confidence. Work on your body, your health, work to achieve a lifestyle that others aspire to, and keep up with yourself. Share your results with others and start to become the person you yourself look up to.

This will not happen overnight. It's a process. The best way to get started is to start creating habits in your life. These habits will become your rituals and in turn, you'll start to get results and attract others.

It's not going to be easy. Your mind will try to stop you from achieving what you want; you'll want to be lazy and not do the work. But you have to have a purpose behind what you're doing or you won't last. And this is why mindset is so important.

In order to be the best and be disciplined, you have to work regardless of what your mind tells you to do. Your mind wants to keep you safe, so it tries to get you to do what is most comfortable. But if you're able to push through and do things consistently, you'll be successful.

There will be many days you don't feel like doing what you need to do. But your feelings have nothing to do with it. You have to work through it, don't let your emotions get in the way of your dreams.

If you become a better leader, your team will surely grow. The more give, the more you attract those who think you can help them. And you will help them because by being a great leader you're able to develop other great leaders who will follow in your footsteps.

Chapter 5: Confidence Building

Because introverts are quiet, they may struggle with their confidence. We can all use more confidence. Even when you've had some success, you may sometimes wonder if you really deserve all the rewards that come along with it.

You do deserve the rewards that come along with this business, and you have to work on your confidence in order to accept and receive gifts; not matter how big or small.

You aren't doing anyone a favor by being broke, lazy, depressed, or weak. In order to truly make a difference in the world, you have to be the best you can and live your life to the fullest.

By being rich, motivated, inspiring, and strong; you inspire others to be the same. This is what will really change the world.

Work On Your Mindset and Belief System

Take time daily to work on your mindset and belief system. Without working on these things it's easy to get off track and forget your purpose for pursuing this business.

You know what they say: Success is 80% mindset and 20% execution. You already know the strategies, you just need to boost your confidence and mindset. You have to believe in what you're doing in order to be successful.

The best way to increase your confidence is to implement

what you learn immediately after learning it. If you learn a new strategy, take action on it consistently until you see results. Once you get the motivation to get started, you feel better like you're accomplishing something, and you'll get the feeling of productivity.

Make sure you're constantly reading or listening to books. Books can be very inspiring and motivating and they can put you in a mindset to want to achieve. But you must take action on what's in the book. Reading is great, but the action is what will make you rich.

Another thing you can do is listen to podcasts, look for podcasts related to personal development, network marketing, and business. These will help you to learn new strategies and work on yourself. If you keep listening to positive things, you're bound to become more knowledgeable and be able to take your business and life to the next level.

Last but not least, to work on your mindset make sure you're always studying the industry: network marketing. Study the top leaders, not only listen to what they say but look at what they're doing. Develop the same habits and routines as them. Do more of what they do, not what they say.

You can find information about network marketing almost anywhere: blogs, books, podcasts, events, etc. Just make sure that you know all about your company, its products, its history, and network marketing as an industry in general.

Work Out

Most of the top leaders that you know are most likely in shape. You don't have to be a supermodel, but you should be healthy. After all, what's the point of building a network marketing empire if you're not around to enjoy it?

Take your health seriously, your health should never come second to anything. Create a habit of working out. You can go to the gym or work out from home. Working out has many benefits, and you most likely already know what they are.

The best time to workout is in the morning, this allows you to get your workout out of the way and continue your day with productivity. If you get bored with the gym, consider going to group exercises classes; this will make your workouts more fun, and you can also meet some friends and possibly some accountability partners.

Dress Better

When you look better, you feel better. Start dressing in a way that you love to see yourself. This will help you to increase confidence. When going to events, make sure to dress up; it'll make you feel better and people will take you more seriously when they see you take time on your appearance.

It's important to pamper yourself and look good. It may sound shallow, but it's proven to increase your confidence.

Results

The one thing that is guaranteed to boost your confidence is results. When you take action and get results, your confidence will soar! Results help you to see what works and where you should be putting your efforts.

Once you do get results, make sure to share them with others in order to attract others. Also, share how you achieved the results.

No result is too small to share, rather it's a new team member, a new customer, or even a new lead. Let others know what you're up to.

Rewards

In order to stay motivated you and give you more confidence, reward yourself. You can do daily rewards, weekly rewards, or even monthly rewards. But you want to get in the habit of rewarding yourself for positive reinforcement.

Positive reinforcement motivates you to take action in order to get more and more rewards. The rewards can be small or big; they can cost money or be free. Whatever makes you happy, and whatever is worth working hard for.

Sometimes you cannot plan for a reward. Sometimes you get results that you didn't expect and it calls for a celebration. Do not delay, celebrate that same day or the very next day. You don't want to delay it or you'll never get around to it.

Rejection

There is one thing that is certain in this business, and its rejection. Keep in mind that people are not necessarily rejecting you, their rejecting the business opportunity or product that you've shared with them.

It's not that they don't trust you, it can be a variety of factors of why people don't want to join or buy. Don't take it personally, keep it moving. Rejection can have a negative effect on your confidence.

In order to stay confident and bounce back from

rejection, you have to have a go-to method for when things get really bad. A place or thing you can do or go to escape and focus on positivity.

Don't allow any one moment to linger in your mind; it's time to move on. Think about where you'll be five years from now if you don't give up. Think about all the lives you can change if you continue to work on yourself and your business daily.

Chapter 6: Creating Goals and a Plan for Success

How will you know where you're headed without goals? Goals are the roadmap that you'll need to stay excited and stay on course. Without goals, you're aimlessly working without a purpose and a mission; which is a disaster within itself.

You have to plan for what you want. You have to design the life that you want. You have to set goals and crush them to get where you want to go.

You may have an idea of what you want. You may just want money right now. But get clear on what you want. Why do you want money? How much money do you want? What will you spend the money on? Clarity is power. Once you know what you're aiming for you begin to live on purpose and with purpose.

Going Forward

Get out a sheet of paper, because we are going to figure out what you want so you'll have a better chance of getting it. I have a question for you: What will you do going forward to achieve your goals?

What is your strategy to get new leads, customers, and recruits? If you don't know that answer then it's time to start doing some research on how to do so.

Once you get the new leads, customers, and recruits; how will you retain them? You have to have a plan to keep them around.

Daily Routine

What actions can you take daily in order to move your business forward? Your daily routine should include things like:

- following up with customers and potential team members
- showing your presentation to "x" amount of people
- training your team
- making phone calls or sending emails
- setting up systems and creating content that will help you to generate more leads
- etc.

Everything else can come secondary. Bagging customer orders and organizing your desk are not income producing activities. Your daily routine should consist of the things that will move your business forward.

Setting Goals

Now it's time to set some goals. I like to break my goals down into weekly goals. But first you have to start with the yearly goal.

For example: Goal #1: I will easily create 300 videos that relate to network marketing by December 31, 2015.

Notice how this goal does not say "I will easily recruit 300 reps". This is because your goals should not be result oriented, but process oriented. If you have result oriented goals, such as monetary goals, you'll get discouraged in the process.

There are some factors you cannot control, and all you can do is implement the strategies you know with quality and hope to see results. You'll most likely get results, but sometimes they can vary.

By setting a yearly goal, you're able to easily create monthly goals. To continue with the example; the monthly goal would be to create 25 videos a month (300 videos/12 months), and the weekly goal would be to create 6 videos a week (25 videos a month/ 4 weeks in a month).

So make sure to break your goals down so that you know what direction to go in, and you'll always know what you should be working on daily and weekly.

If you're trying to make your goal into a habit, make sure to only focus on a few goals for the day; in order to develop a new habit successfully, you shouldn't try to start off with more than three or you'll get overwhelmed and nothing will get done.

Also, keep in mind to work smarter. That means it may be better to do batching for your videos and other content creation. Batching is when you create a whole bunch of content in one sitting. So instead of creating one video a day, you would create all 6 videos in one sitting to get them done for the week.

Taking Action

This is the most important section of this book. Your worth ethic will determine your success above all other things. If you're lazy and you don't spend your time wisely, then you're not going to go anywhere fast.

Implement things with speed, try not to think too much

about it because you may talk yourself out of things that could have had a great impact on your life and business.

Keep your head in the game and stay motivated. Action starts with belief, this is why mindset is so important. If you don't believe in yourself and that you can be successful in this business, you may not take action, even when you know what you should be doing.

Don't allow fear to hold you back, but at the same time stay true to yourself. If you don't take action for you, do it for your team. If you don't have a team yet, do it so you can get results and in turn, get a team.

Nothing will be handed to you and this business is not easy, so let go of all your excuses and stop the mediocre thinking and mediocre habits. Get yourself a mentor and accountability partner so you know you're doing the right things and going in the right direction.

Moving Forward

Now it's time to put it all together. Have clarity. Clarity is power. When you know what you want you can start putting an action plan in place to achieve it.

It's time to use your introversion as a benefit. Own who you are and find ways to do things out of your comfort zone so you can grow. Remember that practice creates confidence. Work on yourself and give network marketing all you've got.

This is a great business. You'll meet new people, have a new experience, and get out of your comfort zone.

Conclusion

Thank you again for reading *Network Marketing For Introverts*!

I hope this book was able to help you to find alternative ways to grow your business.

The next step is to put what you've learned into this book into action!

Finally, if you enjoyed this book, then I'd like to ask you for a favor, would you be kind enough to leave a review for this book on Amazon? It'd be greatly appreciated!

Your review will help other networkers to find the book, it will also give me feedback on what I've done well and what I can improve on.

Thank you and good luck!

Preview of 'Network Marketing Mindset'

Chapter 1: Believe In Yourself and Your Business

Believing in yourself sounds easy, but it's one of the hardest things to do. This is because today there is so much competition and it seems like you'll never get a piece of the pie.

But what you have to realize is, there's always going to be someone better than you at something.

Don't ever waste your time trying to compare yourself to others. It's okay to model them in order to strive for what they have, but it's never okay to compare yourself.

You don't know what it took to achieve what they have. Maybe they have more time than you, maybe they don't have any kids, maybe they work 15 hour days, you just never know.

Don't compare their situation to yours. You also don't know how long they've been doing what they're doing.

When you look at successful network marketers, you don't see the late nights, the studying, and skill building it took for them to get to where they are.

They may have poured hundreds and thousands of dollars into their education. You just don't know-- so don't compare.

To believe in yourself you have to learn to stop comparing yourself and start working on yourself.

You can start by asking yourself the most important question: "Is network marketing right for me?"

Network marketing does have a ton of benefits but realize that it's a people business and you have to depend on people in order to make money.

Also, realize you don't have a lot of control of your business, your company can change the compensation plan at any time.

But one thing does remain the same, you can earn as much as you want. There is not a cap. Also, the start up cost is low, and you gain confidence by interacting with others.

There are many pros and cons, but are you down for whatever is yet to come? Are you willing to deal with people quitting and your company changing its policies?

If so, you believe in your business and the business model.

If you can get past the negatives you can move forward.

Do you believe in yourself? Do you believe you have what it takes to be successful in life?

If not, what's holding you back?

If you're reading this book you need encouragement. Daily!

Start taking your mindset seriously. Do what it takes to start thinking and acting like someone of value.

You can start believing in yourself by accomplishing something. Set a goal to recruit at least one person by next week.

If you achieve this goal, your belief will skyrocket.

But you need more than a goal, you need a plan.

Start investing in books and courses about network marketing. Take yourself seriously and your business seriously.

Once you learn the skills your confidence will increase.

Get yourself organized. Stop playing games, and get out there and do the best you can with what you have!

Don't let anyone tell you you're not good enough. Ignore the people who tell you that this business isn't worth doing.

Ignore the people who aren't on the same track as you. It's time to let go of some of those relationships that are dragging you down. And you know which ones I'm talking about.

You're only as good as you feel. Start taking better care of your body.

Be the best you. Wake up early and go to sleep late.

Having success is going to take sacrifice.

This means no T.V. (especially the news), no video games, no senseless spending, no vacations.

If you truly want to reach your goals, give up some of the things that are wasting your time.

Become more of a productive person.

Start saying yes to the things that will make you a better person. Like seminars, working out, and eating healthy.

Get out of your comfort zone and start being more serious and disciplined.

Check out the rest of Network Marketing Mindset on Amazon

Check Out My Other Books

Below you'll find some of my other popular books that are popular on Amazon and Kindle as well. You can visit my author page on Amazon to see other work done by me.

How To Get Customers In Your Network Marketing Company: The Complete Guide To Converting Leads Into Loyal Customers

Internet Marketing For Network Marketers: How To Create Automated Systems To Get Recruits and Customers Online

Network Marketing Mindset: Personal Development and Confidence Building For Network Marketers

Network Marketing Selling Secrets: 50 Ways To Get New Customers

Bonus Video: How To Get Leads and Customers Online

Subscribe To Get Free Tips On How To Generate Leads and Get Customers

When you subscribe to get network marketing tips via email, you will get free access to exclusive subscriber-only resources. All you have to do is enter your email address to the right to get instant access.

These resources will help you get more out of your business – to be able to reach your goals, have more motivation, be at your best, and live the life you've always dreamed of. I'm always adding new resources, which you will be notified of as a subscriber. These will help you get an endless amount of leads and customers.

Visit http://www.networkmarketingkingdom.com/video to Acces The Bonus Video

Printed in Great Britain
by Amazon